Lou Flew Too!

Pam Scheunemann

Consulting Editor, Diane Craig, M.A./Reading Specialist

ABDO
Publishing Company

Published by ABDO Publishing Company, 4940 Viking Drive, Edina, Minnesota 55435.

Printed in the United States.

Credits
Edited by: Pam Price
Curriculum Coordinator: Nancy Tuminelly
Cover and Interior Design and Production: Mighty Media
Photo and Illustration Credits: BananaStock Ltd., Brand X Pictures, Corbis Images, Digital Vision, Hemera, Image Source, Tracy Kompelien, PhotoDisc, Stockbyte

Library of Congress Cataloging-in-Publication Data

Scheunemann, Pam, 1955-
    Lou flew too! / Pam Scheunemann.
      p. cm. -- (Rhyme time)
    Includes index.
    ISBN 1-59197-803-3 (hardcover)
    ISBN 1-59197-909-9 (paperback)
    1. English language--Rhyme--Juvenile literature. I. Title. II. Rhyme time (ABDO Publishing Company)

PE1517.S43 2004
428.1'3--dc22

                                                                    2004047351

SandCastle™ books are created by a professional team of educators, reading specialists, and content developers around five essential components that include phonemic awareness, phonics, vocabulary, text comprehension, and fluency. All books are written, reviewed, and leveled for guided reading, early intervention reading, and Accelerated Reader® programs and designed for use in shared, guided, and independent reading and writing activities to support a balanced approach to literacy instruction.

Let Us Know

After reading the book, SandCastle would like you to tell us your stories about reading. What is your favorite page? Was there something hard that you needed help with? Share the ups and downs of learning to read. We want to hear from you! To get posted on the ABDO Publishing Company Web site, send us e-mail at:

sandcastle@abdopub.com

SandCastle Level: Fluent

Words that rhyme do not have to be spelled the same. These words rhyme with each other:

blew

hue

due

knew

flew

through

glue

too

hairdo

true

Sean works to finish the
assignment before it is **due**.

To make a lot of bubbles, Fay and Heather blew hard.

Sierra, Ally, and their mom **glue** paper hearts together to make Valentine's Day cards.

Violet and Daisy have the same hairdo.

Trina is painting some flowers.

She paints the petals a pinkish hue.

Isaiah and his dad held on to the string as their kite **flew**.

Madeline thinks the tunnel is fun to crawl through.

Gavin studied hard for the test, so he **knew** that he would do well.

Aidan and his dad are reading a **true** story.

It is Jackson's turn on the swing.

When he is done, Zachary and Benjamin will get to swing too.

Lou Flew Too!

There was a duck named Lou.
He had a cool hairdo.

One day a cool breeze blew through.

Lou noticed the leaves
had changed hue.

He knew that winter was due.

Lou had a slew
of friends who were true.

17

Lou and his crew
stuck together like glue.

So when Lou packed up,
his crew did too!

They didn't even have to think it through.

And off toward the south they flew!

Rhyming Riddle

What do you call
the color of someone's hairstyle?

Hairdo hue

Glossary

assignment. work given to someone to complete

crew. a group of people joined together by common work or common interests

due. the time at which something is scheduled to arrive or happen

hue. a color or a shade of a color

slew. a lot

About SandCastle™

A professional team of educators, reading specialists, and content developers created the SandCastle™ series to support young readers as they develop reading skills and strategies and increase their general knowledge. The SandCastle™ series has four levels that correspond to early literacy development in young children. The levels are provided to help teachers and parents select the appropriate books for young readers.

Emerging Readers
(no flags)

Beginning Readers
(1 flag)

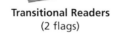

Transitional Readers
(2 flags)

Fluent Readers
(3 flags)

These levels are meant only as a guide. All levels are subject to change.

ABDO
Publishing Company

To see a complete list of SandCastle™ books and other nonfiction titles from ABDO Publishing Company, visit **www.abdopub.com** or contact us at: 4940 Viking Drive, Edina, Minnesota 55435 • 1-800-800-1312 • fax: 1-952-831-1632